Quail Keeping in the UK: A Comprehen

Hobbyists and Smallholder

2023

Introduction:
Introduce quail as an increasingly popular option for poultry enthusiasts in the UK.

- Discuss the benefits of raising quail and their versatility in various settings.
- Explain your purpose in writing the book and what readers can expect to learn.

Chapter 1: Understanding Quail Species Suitable for the UK

- Overview of quail species commonly raised in the UK (Coturnix, Bobwhite, etc.).
- Climate considerations and how they affect quail keeping choices.
- Selecting the right quail breed for different purposes (eggs, meat, pets).

Chapter 2: Legalities and Regulations in the UK

- Discuss the legal requirements for keeping quail in the UK.
- Permits and licenses, if applicable.
- Compliance with animal welfare standards and best practices.

Chapter 3: Housing and Enclosure Setup

- Building or choosing suitable quail housing for the UK climate.
- Proper ventilation and insulation for varying seasons.
- Designing quail-friendly enclosures to promote natural behaviour.

Chapter 4: Feeding and Nutrition for Healthy Quail

- Understanding quail dietary needs in the UK.
- Local feed options and supplements.

- Tips for providing a balanced and nutritious diet.

Chapter 5: Health Care and Disease Prevention
- Common health issues specific to quail in the UK.
- Recognising signs of illness and when to seek veterinary care.
- Implementing biosecurity measures to prevent disease outbreaks.

Chapter 6: Breeding and Incubation in the UK
- Breeding strategies for successful reproduction.
- Seasonal considerations for breeding in the UK.
- Incubation techniques and best practices.

Chapter 7: Maximising Quail Egg Production
- Tips for optimising egg production in the UK climate.
- Extending the laying season through husbandry practices.
- Handling and storing quail eggs for freshness.

Chapter 8: Utilising Quail Meat in the UK
- Humanely raising quail for meat in the UK.
- Slaughtering and processing quail for the table.
- Preparing traditional and innovative quail meat dishes.

Chapter 9: Quail as Pets and Educational Resources
- Quail as pets in the UK: Care and interaction.
- Incorporating quail into educational programs and school projects.
- Promoting awareness of quail as a sustainable option in the UK.

Chapter 10: Troubleshooting and FAQs for UK Quail Keepers
- Addressing common challenges faced by UK quail keepers.
- Frequently asked questions and practical solutions.

Troubleshooting and FAQ

Conclusion:

Appendix:
- List of UK-specific resources, organisations, and forums for quail enthusiasts.
- Glossary of terms relevant to UK quail keeping.

About the author

Meet Chris Wolf: The Quail Enthusiast

Chris Wolf is a passionate and experienced quail keeper, renowned for his expertise in raising these captivating birds. Born and raised in the scenic countryside of the United Kingdom, Chris developed a deep appreciation for nature and its wonders from a young age. As he matured, his fascination with wildlife and sustainable living led him to explore the world of poultry keeping, ultimately finding his true calling in raising quail.

With over a decade of hands-on experience, Chris has become a respected authority in the quail-keeping community. His journey began with a small flock of Coturnix quail, and his fascination quickly grew as he witnessed their remarkable adaptability and diverse personalities. Over the years, he has expanded his quail family to include various species, from the beloved Coturnix to the charming Bobwhite and elegant California quail.

Through dedication and a thirst for knowledge, Chris has honed his skills in providing top-notch care for his quail. His expertise extends to all aspects of quail keeping, from selecting the ideal breed for specific purposes to designing comfortable and predator-proof enclosures. Chris is also well-versed in creating balanced diets for his birds, ensuring optimal egg production and healthy growth.

Chris's genuine love for his quail is evident in his daily interactions with them. He takes great joy in observing their unique behaviours and nurturing their well-being. His gentle and patient approach has earned him a reputation as a quail whisperer, as his birds show trust and comfort in his presence.

Being an advocate for ethical and sustainable practices, Chris has mastered the art of raising quail humanely for both eggs and meat. He firmly believes that providing a happy and stress-free life for his quail directly translates into the superior quality of their products.

Beyond his personal quail-keeping endeavours, Chris is dedicated to sharing his vast knowledge with others. He regularly hosts workshops, gives talks at local poultry clubs, and actively participates in online forums to help fellow enthusiasts. His dream is to inspire and empower individuals from all walks of life to embrace quail keeping as a rewarding and environmentally conscious hobby or even a sustainable food source.

Importance of self sufficiency

In a world of constant change and uncertainty, self-sufficiency has become increasingly important. Self-sufficiency refers to the ability of individuals, families, and communities to meet their basic needs independently, without relying heavily on external sources or systems. This concept has gained significance for several reasons.

Resilience in Times of Crisis:
The world is no stranger to unexpected crises, whether they be natural disasters, economic downturns, or global pandemics. Being self-sufficient ensures that individuals and communities have the resources and skills to withstand such challenges and continue functioning even when external support is limited or disrupted.

Reduced Vulnerability to Supply Chain Disruptions:
In today's interconnected world, supply chains are complex and often global. Relying heavily on external sources for basic necessities can make individuals and nations vulnerable to disruptions in these supply chains. Self-sufficiency allows for

greater control over essential resources, reducing dependence on distant suppliers.

Environmental Sustainability:

Embracing self-sufficiency often involves adopting sustainable practices that minimise environmental impact. By reducing reliance on mass-produced goods and opting for local, eco-friendly alternatives, individuals contribute to environmental preservation and combat climate change.

Personal Empowerment and Sense of Achievement:

Achieving self-sufficiency instils a sense of empowerment and pride in one's abilities. When individuals can grow their food, generate renewable energy, or create useful products, they experience a profound sense of accomplishment and independence.

Preserving Traditional Knowledge and Skills:

As societies modernise, traditional knowledge and skills are at risk of being lost. Self-sufficiency encourages the preservation of age-old practices related to farming, handicrafts, and sustainable living, passing on valuable knowledge to future generations.

Enhancing Community Cohesion:
Self-sufficiency often fosters stronger community ties. Local bartering and trading, sharing surplus resources, and collective problem-solving build a sense of solidarity among community members, leading to stronger, more resilient communities.

Adaptability to Economic Uncertainty:
In times of economic uncertainty or job instability, self-sufficiency can provide a safety net. Having the means to grow food, generate income through small-scale ventures, or reduce expenses through resourceful practices can ease financial burdens during difficult times.

Cultivating Independence from Consumer Culture:
Modern society often promotes a consumer-driven culture, where individuals are encouraged to buy more and depend on commercial products and services. Self-sufficiency

encourages a shift away from this consumerism, emphasising mindful consumption and minimal waste.

Empowering Rural Development:

In rural areas, self-sufficiency is a powerful tool for sustainable development. By utilising local resources and skills, rural communities can thrive economically and maintain their cultural heritage.

A Path to a More Sustainable Future:

As the world grapples with issues such as climate change, resource depletion, and population growth, embracing self-sufficiency offers a path toward a more sustainable future. It encourages individuals and societies to live in harmony with the environment and prioritise long-term well-being over short-term gains.

While complete self-sufficiency may not be achievable or desirable for everyone, striving to become more self-reliant in various aspects of life can have far-reaching benefits. Embracing self-sufficiency fosters a sense of responsibility, adaptability, and mindfulness, making individuals and communities better equipped to face an ever-changing world with resilience and optimism.

In addition to his practical wisdom, Chris is a firm advocate for promoting awareness of quail as educational resources in schools and communities. He firmly believes that nurturing an understanding of these fascinating birds will instil a deeper respect for nature and responsible animal care in future generations.

Through his journey as a quail enthusiast, Chris Wolf has not only enriched his own life but also the lives of countless others. His passion for quail keeping, dedication to their well-being, and unwavering commitment to sharing his knowledge in this book.

Quail Keeping in the UK: A Comprehensive Guide for Hobbyists and Homesteaders

Quail, once a lesser-known bird in the world of poultry, has risen to become an increasingly popular option for poultry enthusiasts in the United Kingdom. These small, captivating birds offer a wealth of benefits that appeal to a diverse range of individuals, from hobbyists seeking a rewarding pastime to homesteaders searching for a sustainable source of eggs and meat. In this comprehensive guide, we delve into the fascinating world of quail keeping, shedding light on the many advantages these birds bring to the table and their incredible adaptability in various settings.

Discover the Versatility of Quail:

Quail, those captivating and versatile birds, possess a unique set of attributes that render them exceptionally well-suited for a multitude of purposes. Their remarkable adaptability and diverse array of offerings make them an ideal choice for enthusiasts across various domains. Be it their endearing companionship as pets, the bountiful yield of nutrition-packed eggs they bestow, or the delectable, tender meat they provide, quail undoubtedly showcase a spectrum of advantages that cater to a spectrum of needs and desires.

The world of quail keeping opens up a treasure trove of possibilities, each tailored to an individual's preferences and requirements. For those seeking the companionship of feathered friends, quail emerge as charming pets that offer a unique and delightful presence. Their petite size, vibrant plumage, and engaging antics make them captivating to watch, filling every corner of their environment with liveliness. Their charming behaviours, like their endearing waddling gait, synchronised movements, and social interactions, have the power to bring joy and amusement to both novice and seasoned keepers alike.

Yet, quail's appeal goes far beyond their charismatic personalities. These birds are renowned for their exceptional egg production, delivering a constant supply of small but nutrient-dense eggs that are a culinary treasure. Packed with essential proteins, vitamins, and minerals, quail eggs offer a nutritionally potent alternative to their larger counterparts.

Their relatively smaller size lends them a unique charm, and they find themselves adorning breakfast plates, hors d'oeuvres, and gourmet dishes, offering a delectable and aesthetically pleasing addition to a variety of culinary creations.

Moreover, quail extend their offerings to gastronomic delights with their succulent and flavourful meat. Especially in the case of specific breeds, such as the Jumbo Quail, their larger size makes them a prime choice for meat production. The meat is noted for its tender texture and distinctive taste, earning it a place in gourmet cuisines that seek exceptional flavour profiles.

Beyond their roles as companions and culinary contributors, quail are also admired for their resourcefulness. They exhibit a natural propensity for thriving in diverse environments, adapting to various housing conditions and dietary options. This adaptability, combined with their relatively low space requirements, makes them accessible even to urban dwellers with limited outdoor areas.

In conclusion, quail are not merely birds; they are a source of multifaceted marvel. Their versatility encompasses the realm of pets, gourmet cuisine, and resourceful companions in a manner that few other avian species can match. Their captivating behaviours bring joy, their eggs and meat elevate culinary experiences, and their adaptability allows them to grace a wide range of settings. As you embark on the journey of quail keeping, be prepared to discover a world of possibilities that these remarkable birds effortlessly unfold before you.

Benefits of Raising Quail:

One of the most enticing aspects of raising quail is their manageable size, which sets them apart from larger poultry species like chickens or ducks. Their smaller footprint makes them a fantastic alternative for those with limited space, allowing them to thrive in urban backyards, suburban gardens, and even rural homesteads without overwhelming the available area.

Moreover, quail are renowned for their rapid growth and early maturity, which translates to efficient resource utilisation in terms of time and resources. For those interested in eggs, quail lay eggs prolifically and at an early age. Each Coturnix quail, also known as Japanese quail, can lay up to an impressive 300 eggs per year, providing a reliable and efficient source of fresh, nutritious eggs.

Quail meat has also gained popularity among health-conscious consumers due to its tenderness and low-fat content. Raising quail for meat production offers a sustainable and tasty source of lean quail meat, and these birds can reach a desirable size for meat production within 6-8 weeks.

Additionally, quail's amiable nature makes them an excellent choice for families and children interested in poultry-keeping without the intimidating size of larger birds. Their friendly and calm demeanour makes them easy to handle and interact with, making them an ideal choice for poultry enthusiasts of all ages.

Our Purpose in Writing this Book:

As avid quail enthusiasts ourselves, we have experienced the joy and fulfilment that comes from keeping these wonderful birds. However, we also understand that diving into the world of quail keeping can be daunting for beginners. Our purpose in writing this book is to provide a comprehensive and accessible resource for individuals interested in keeping quail in the UK.

Whether you're an urban dweller with limited experience in poultry-keeping or a seasoned homesteader seeking to expand your flock, this guide is designed to walk you through every step of the quail-keeping journey. From selecting the right quail breed for your needs to providing the best care and ensuring their well-being, we aim to equip you with the knowledge and confidence to successfully raise quail and reap the rewards they bring.

What to Expect:

Throughout the chapters that follow, we will explore various facets of quail keeping, each dedicated to addressing the specific aspects of raising quail in the UK. You will gain valuable insights into selecting the right quail species suitable for your environment, setting up their housing to accommodate the UK climate, providing optimal nutrition, managing their health and breeding, and even utilising their eggs and meat.

Moreover, we will tackle legalities and regulations to ensure that your quail keeping endeavours comply with the UK's animal welfare standards and requirements. Troubleshooting common challenges and answering frequently asked questions will ensure that you are well-prepared to overcome any obstacles that may arise.

By the end of this guide, we hope you will not only feel empowered to embark on your quail-keeping adventure but also appreciate the significance of quail in sustainable and ethical poultry practices. Let's journey together into the fascinating world of quail keeping and unlock the rewards these captivating birds have to offer.

Chapter 1: Understanding Quail Species Suitable for the UK

Quail keeping in the United Kingdom has gained significant traction in recent years, and for good reason. The charming and versatile quail species offer a rewarding experience for poultry enthusiasts of all levels, from backyard hobbyists to experienced homesteaders. In this chapter, we delve deeper into the quail species commonly raised in the UK, taking into account the unique climate considerations that impact quail-keeping choices. Furthermore, we explore the process of selecting the right quail breed based on various purposes, including egg production, meat, and keeping them as delightful pets.

Overview of Quail Species Commonly Raised in the UK:

Coturnix Quail (Japanese Quail): Coturnix quail are undoubtedly the darlings of the UK quail-keeping scene. These small, hardy birds are renowned for their prolific egg-laying abilities, producing small, speckled eggs that are prized for their rich flavour. Coturnix quail mature quickly, reaching their laying age as early as 6-8 weeks. With proper care, each

Coturnix quail can lay up to an impressive 300 eggs per year, making them a reliable and efficient source of fresh, nutritious eggs.

Bobwhite Quail: While slightly less common than Coturnix quail, Bobwhite quail have their own devoted following in the UK. These birds are appreciated for their delightful and distinct "bob-white" calls, which add a touch of natural music to any quail-keeping setup. Bobwhite quail may require more space and attention compared to Coturnix quail, but their charming personalities and distinctive markings make them a favourite among enthusiasts seeking a unique quail-keeping experience.

California Quail: Although less frequently raised in the UK due to their specific housing and care requirements, California quail hold a special appeal for those interested in keeping quail as pets or adding ornamental beauty to their aviaries. With their striking plumage and sociable behaviour, California quail are captivating to watch and can create a charming atmosphere in any outdoor setting.

Climate Considerations and Quail Keeping Choices:

The United Kingdom's climate varies significantly from region to region, but overall, it is characterised by mild temperatures with relatively high humidity and frequent rainfall. As quail are hardy birds, they can generally adapt to a range of conditions, but understanding the climate's impact on quail-keeping choices is crucial for ensuring their well-being and productivity.

Temperature Tolerance: Coturnix quail are well-suited for the UK's temperate climate, with their tolerance for cooler temperatures. However, providing appropriate shelter is essential, as quails can be susceptible to drafts and extreme cold. On the other hand, California quail may require additional protection during colder months due to their preference for warmer environments.

Dampness Management: Given the United Kingdom's frequently damp climate, the well-being of quails can be significantly impacted by the challenges posed by excess moisture. These birds are particularly susceptible to respiratory problems when subjected to prolonged periods of high humidity and dampness. To address this issue and ensure optimal quail health, it becomes imperative to implement effective dampness management strategies.

A crucial aspect of mitigating the adverse effects of damp conditions on quail health is to provide appropriate housing that prioritises ventilation and dryness. Proper airflow within the quail housing not only prevents the accumulation of moisture but also helps regulate the internal environment. Adequate ventilation ensures that the air quality remains high, reducing the risk of respiratory distress among the quails. By promoting air exchange, potential airborne contaminants and excess humidity are effectively expelled from the living space, creating an environment that supports the quails' respiratory well-being.

Maintaining dryness within the quail housing is essential for preventing the proliferation of mould, bacteria, and other harmful pathogens that thrive in damp conditions. The presence of these microorganisms can significantly compromise the quails' health, leading to infections and other ailments. Regular cleaning routines and the prompt removal of damp bedding can play a pivotal role in minimising the moisture content in the environment. Additionally, choosing appropriate bedding materials is vital, as certain materials have superior moisture-absorbing properties, effectively reducing dampness within the quail living space.

Providing suitable bedding material is another key component of effective dampness management. The choice of bedding should take into account its ability to absorb moisture while maintaining a comfortable and hygienic space for the quails. Wood shavings, straw, or similar materials with moisture-wicking properties are excellent options to consider. These materials not only help keep the quails dry by drawing away excess moisture from the environment but also provide a soft and insulated surface for them to rest on.

Creating a holistic approach to dampness management involves a combination of well-ventilated housing, appropriate bedding materials, and vigilant maintenance practices. By ensuring that the quail housing remains dry, clean, and adequately ventilated, quail owners can significantly reduce the risks associated with respiratory issues and other health challenges caused by excessive humidity. This proactive approach not only promotes the overall well-being of the quails but also fosters an environment conducive to their growth, productivity, and long-term vitality in the often damp climate of the UK.

Selecting the Right Quail Breed for Different Purposes:

Egg Production: For those seeking a steady supply of delicious and nutritious eggs, Coturnix quail are the go-to choice. Their remarkable egg-laying capacity and early maturity make them highly efficient egg producers, making them the preferred breed for egg-centric quail keeping.
Quail eggs, though diminutive in size, pack a powerful nutritional punch that belies their appearance. These petite treasures are teeming with a remarkable array of essential nutrients that contribute to overall health and well-being. Here's a closer look at the nutritional benefits of quail eggs:

1. Protein Powerhouse Quail eggs are a concentrated source of high-quality protein. Their protein content is comparable to that of chicken eggs, but due to their smaller size, they offer a more convenient and easily portioned protein boost. Protein is crucial for muscle repair and growth, immune function, and the production of enzymes and hormones.

2. Rich in Vitamins Quail eggs are rich in several essential vitamins, including vitamin A, B-vitamins (such as B1, B2, B6, and B12), and vitamin D. Vitamin A supports vision, skin health, and immune function, while B-vitamins are vital for energy metabolism, nervous system health, and overall vitality. Vitamin D is important for bone health, immune function, and aiding in the absorption of calcium.

3. Mineral Bounty These eggs are a notable source of minerals like iron, phosphorus, and zinc. Iron is crucial for transporting oxygen throughout the body and preventing anaemia, while phosphorus is essential for bone health, energy production, and cellular function. Zinc supports immune function, wound healing, and proper growth.

4. Healthy Fats Quail eggs contain healthy fats, including monounsaturated and polyunsaturated fats. These fats are heart-healthy and contribute to overall cardiovascular well-being. They also play a role in brain health, hormone production, and the absorption of fat-soluble vitamins.

5. Choline Content Choline, a vital nutrient often grouped with B-vitamins, is abundant in quail eggs. Choline is essential for brain development, nerve function, and the metabolism of fats. It also supports liver health and aids in maintaining a healthy cardiovascular system.

6. Complete Amino Acid Profile The protein in quail eggs boasts a complete range of amino acids, making it a valuable protein source. Amino acids are the building blocks of proteins and are necessary for various physiological processes, including tissue repair, immune function, and the production of enzymes and hormones.

7. Lower Allergen Risk Quail eggs are considered to have a lower allergenic potential compared to chicken eggs. This

makes them a potentially suitable option for individuals who are sensitive to chicken egg proteins.

8. Bioavailability The nutrients in quail eggs are easily digestible and have high bioavailability, meaning that the body can efficiently absorb and utilize these nutrients for optimal health benefits.

9. Weight Management Quail eggs can be a beneficial addition to weight management plans due to their protein content, which helps promote satiety and regulate appetite. Additionally, their nutrient density provides essential nutrients without a high caloric load.

Incorporating quail eggs into your diet can provide a variety of health benefits. Their unique nutrient composition and culinary versatility make them a valuable addition to a balanced and nutritious diet.

Meat Production: When it comes to meat production, Coturnix quail shine yet again. They grow rapidly and can reach a desirable size for meat production within 6-8 weeks, providing a sustainable and tasty source of lean quail meat. However, if you have ample space and are willing to invest more time and care, Bobwhite quail can also be raised for their delectable meat.

Pets and Aviary Birds: If your quail-keeping goals revolve around having delightful pets or ornamental birds for your aviary, California quail and Bobwhite quail are excellent choices. Their attractive appearances and charming behaviours make them enjoyable companions, adding a touch of elegance to your outdoor space.

Sexing quail can be a bit challenging, especially when they are young, as they do not have significant visual differences between males and females. However, as they mature, some quail species develop certain characteristics that can help you determine their sex. Here are some methods to sex quail:

1. Physical Differences: In some quail species, males and females may have subtle differences in size and plumage. For example, male Coturnix quail (Japanese quail) tend to have a

slightly larger and more pronounced cloacal vent (located under the tail) compared to females. Additionally, some males may have a slightly bolder and darker coloration than females.

2. Vocalisation: In some species, male quail may have a distinct and louder call compared to females. For example, male Bobwhite quail have a characteristic "bob-white" call, while females produce a softer call.

3. Behaviour: Observing the behaviour of quail can also provide clues about their sex. In some species, males may display more aggressive behaviour, such as chasing or fighting with other males, especially during the breeding season.

4. Cloacal Examination: As quail mature, the cloacal region of males and females may show some differences. However, this method requires experience and expertise, as it can be tricky to identify these differences accurately.

5. DNA Sexing: If you need to be absolutely sure of the sex of your quail, you can use DNA sexing. This method involves collecting a small blood sample or feather from the quail and sending it to a laboratory for analysis. DNA sexing is highly accurate but can be more expensive than other methods.

Keep in mind that the methods mentioned above may not be foolproof, especially with young quail. As they mature, it becomes easier to identify their sex. If you plan to breed quail, it's essential to have a balanced ratio of males to females for successful reproduction. If unsure about the sex of your quail, it's a good idea to seek advice from experienced quail keepers or a veterinarian with avian expertise.

In conclusion, understanding the various quail species suitable for the UK is crucial for making informed decisions in quail keeping. Each quail species brings its unique attributes and requirements, allowing you to tailor your quail-keeping experience to suit your preferences and specific purposes. Whether you aspire to savour fresh quail eggs, relish the delicious quail meat, or simply enjoy the delightful company of quail as pets, the UK offers an ideal environment to embark on a fulfilling and rewarding quail-keeping adventure.

Chapter 2: Legalities and Regulations in the UK

Quail keeping in the United Kingdom is subject to certain legal requirements and regulations to ensure the welfare of the birds and maintain environmental sustainability. This chapter provides an in-depth exploration of the legal aspects involved in keeping quail, including the necessary permits and licenses, if applicable, and emphasises the importance of adhering to animal welfare standards and best practices.

Legal Requirements for Keeping Quail in the UK:

In the UK, quail keeping is governed by various laws and regulations designed to protect the welfare of the birds and prevent potential risks to public health and the environment. Aspiring quail keepers should be aware of the following legal requirements:

Animal Welfare Act 2006: The Animal Welfare Act sets the foundation for animal welfare in the UK. It places a duty of care on animal keepers to ensure the needs of their animals are met, including access to proper shelter, nutrition, water, and a suitable environment to express their natural behaviours.

General License Requirements: Depending on the scale of quail keeping and the specific purpose, you may need to obtain a general license from the relevant authorities. These licenses typically cover activities such as keeping birds in captivity, breeding, selling, or releasing them into the wild.

Transportation of Quail: If you intend to transport quail, you must adhere to specific transportation regulations to ensure the birds' safety and minimise stress during the journey.

Biosecurity Measures: To prevent the spread of diseases, biosecurity measures must be implemented, especially if you have multiple bird species on your premises.

Permits and Licenses, if Applicable:

While keeping quail for personal use or in small numbers may not require a specific license, certain activities may necessitate obtaining permits from the appropriate authorities. These activities include:

Selling Quail Eggs: If you intend to sell quail eggs for human consumption, you may need to register with the local council or obtain a license from the Food Standards Agency (FSA).

Releasing Quail into the Wild: Releasing non-native quail species into the wild is strictly regulated to prevent potential ecological disruptions. It is essential to seek advice from relevant environmental agencies before considering any releases.

Commercial Quail Farming: Commercial quail farming, especially on a large scale, usually requires additional permits and compliance with health and safety regulations. This may include approval from the Animal and Plant Health Agency (APHA) and registration with the Rural Payments Agency (RPA) if claiming agricultural grants.

Compliance with Animal Welfare Standards and Best Practices:

As responsible quail keepers, it is crucial to prioritise the welfare of these birds and provide them with the best possible care. Adhering to animal welfare standards and best practices not only ensures the well-being of the quail but also contributes to the sustainability and success of your quail-keeping venture.

Housing and Space Requirements: Provide adequate space in the quail enclosure to allow the birds to move freely and express their natural behaviours. Ensure shelter from harsh weather conditions and use suitable bedding to maintain a dry and comfortable environment.

Nutrition and Water: Offer a balanced and appropriate diet for quail, ensuring they receive all essential nutrients. Access to clean, fresh water must always be available.

Health Monitoring: Regularly inspect your quail for signs of illness or distress, and promptly seek veterinary attention if needed. Implement biosecurity measures to prevent the introduction and spread of diseases.

Handling and Socialisation: Handle quail gently and minimise stress during routine management practices. Proper socialisation helps quail become more comfortable with human presence and reduces skittish behaviour.

Humane Slaughter: If raising quail for meat, ensure humane slaughter practices are followed to minimise stress and pain for the birds.

Educate Yourself: Stay informed about the latest advancements in quail husbandry, best practices, and any changes in legal requirements.

Conclusion:

Compliance with the legal requirements, permits, and licenses, where applicable, is crucial for quail keepers in the UK. Adhering to these regulations not only ensures that you are keeping quail responsibly but also helps protect the welfare of these charming birds and contributes to environmental sustainability. By prioritising the well-being of your quail and following best practices, you can create a thriving and rewarding quail-keeping experience that benefits both you and your feathered companions.

Chapter 3: Housing and Enclosure Setup for Quail in the UK

Creating a suitable and comfortable housing environment is essential for the well-being and productivity of your quail. In this chapter, we will guide you through building or choosing appropriate quail housing tailored to the unique climate of the United Kingdom. We'll also cover proper ventilation and insulation considerations to ensure your quail are comfortable throughout the changing seasons. Furthermore, we'll explore how to design quail-friendly enclosures that encourage their natural behaviours, promoting a happy and thriving quail flock.

Building or Choosing Suitable Quail Housing for the UK Climate:

The first step in setting up quail housing is deciding whether to build a custom enclosure or purchase a pre-made one. Consider the following factors when making your choice:

Space Requirements: Providing adequate space for quails is a fundamental aspect of their care, particularly when they are unable to roam freely. The amount of space available directly influences their overall well-being, behaviour, and productivity. Calculating the appropriate space requirements for the number of quails you intend to keep is essential to ensure they can move around comfortably and exhibit natural behaviours within their enclosure.

When determining the optimal space for your quails, it's important to consider the specific breed, age, and purpose of raising them. Different quail breeds might have varying space preferences, with some being more active and requiring more room to move around. Additionally, the age of the quails plays a role, as younger birds tend to be more active and require extra space to exercise and explore.

For example, let's consider a scenario where you plan to keep Coturnix quails for egg production. These quails are known for their small size and relatively active nature. If you have a flock of 20 Coturnix quails, a recommended guideline is to provide around 1 square foot of space per quail. This means that for a flock of 20 quails, you would need an enclosure that is at least 20 square feet in size. This space allocation allows the quails to move freely, engage in dust bathing, and exhibit natural behaviours without feeling cramped.

In another instance, if you're raising Bobwhite quails, which are slightly larger and more ground-dwelling in nature, you might want to increase the space allocation. For a flock of 15 Bobwhite quails, you could aim for approximately 2 square feet per bird. This larger space requirement accommodates their need for more ground-level movement and encourages the expression of their natural behaviours.

Furthermore, overcrowding can lead to stress, increased aggression, and a higher risk of disease transmission among quails. Providing ample space not only ensures their physical well-being but also positively impacts their psychological health. Quails that have sufficient room to move, forage, and interact with their environment tend to be calmer, less prone to stress-related issues, and more likely to exhibit their natural behaviours.

To create a comfortable and spacious environment for your quails, consider incorporating features like perches, dust bathing areas, and hiding spots within their enclosure. These elements enrich their living space and promote mental and physical stimulation.

In conclusion, understanding the space requirements for the quail species you intend to raise is crucial for their overall health and happiness. By calculating the appropriate amount of space based on the number of quails in your flock and their specific needs, you create an environment where they can thrive, engage in natural behaviours, and contribute positively to your farming or hobbyist endeavours.

Materials: Use durable, non-toxic materials for construction to ensure the safety and longevity of the housing. Wood and metal are common choices for building quail coops.

Accessibility: Design the housing for easy access to food and water containers, nesting areas, and for cleaning purposes. Quail do poop an awful lot, however, it makes great compost.

Protection: Ensuring the safety and security of your quail is a paramount consideration when setting up their enclosure. The enclosure serves as a fortress that shields the quail from a range of potential threats, including predators, harsh weather, and the spread of diseases. By implementing robust protective measures, you create an environment in which your quail can thrive without constant risk.

Predator Prevention: Predators pose a significant danger to quail, particularly in outdoor enclosures. Various animals, such as foxes, birds of prey, rats and even domestic pets, might view quail as easy prey. To thwart these potential threats, it's imperative to design the enclosure with predator prevention in mind. This might involve constructing a secure perimeter fence, buried partially underground to prevent digging predators from gaining access. The fence should be made from durable materials, such as hardware cloth or welded wire, with small enough gaps to prevent predators from squeezing through. Adding an overhead cover or netting can help deter birds of prey from swooping down.

Example: If you're raising quail in an area known for its fox population, you'd need to erect a sturdy enclosure with both above-ground and below-ground reinforcement. For instance, a wire mesh fence that's at least 4-6 feet tall, buried at least a foot below the ground's surface, and topped with netting would provide multi-layered protection against potential predators.

Extreme Weather Protection: The enclosure should also shield the quail from adverse weather conditions. This includes protecting them from excessive heat, rain, wind, and cold temperatures. Providing shade structures or shelters within the enclosure can help quail find relief from intense sunlight or sudden downpours. Additionally, creating a well-insulated space can help regulate temperature during colder months.

Example: In regions where the climate experiences extreme temperature variations, such as hot summers and cold winters, your quail enclosure could include both shaded areas and insulated shelters. These shelters might be constructed with appropriate materials to provide thermal insulation and protection from the elements.

Disease Prevention: The enclosure should be designed to minimise the risk of disease transmission. Regular cleaning and disinfection are crucial. Additionally, consider biosecurity measures, such as limiting contact between your quail and wild birds, which can carry diseases.

Example: If you're raising quail in an area where avian influenza outbreaks have occurred, you might implement strict biosecurity measures such as disinfecting footwear before entering the enclosure, using separate equipment for handling quail, and restricting access to the enclosure to authorised personnel only.

Secure Latches: Properly securing the enclosure with high-quality latches is essential. This prevents not only predators from entering but also quail from escaping. Quail are agile and can find small openings to slip through, so attention to detail when designing the latches is crucial.

Example: Installing latches that require multiple steps or complex motions can help ensure that quail remain safely contained. Spring-loaded latches that automatically close behind you after entry can prevent accidental escapes due to human error.

In conclusion, the protective aspects of the quail enclosure are multifaceted and require thoughtful consideration. By addressing predator prevention, extreme weather protection, disease prevention, and secure latching mechanisms, you establish an environment that prioritises the quail's safety, well-being, and overall success in your care.

Proper Ventilation and Insulation for Varying Seasons:

The UK climate experiences diverse seasons, ranging from mild and rainy to colder and wetter weather. Providing proper ventilation and insulation in your quail housing is crucial to maintaining a healthy and comfortable environment for your birds:

Ensure adequate ventilation in the quail housing to prevent the buildup of moisture, ammonia, and other harmful gases. Proper air circulation helps maintain air quality and prevents respiratory issues.

Insulation: Insulating the housing can help regulate the temperature, keeping it cooler during hot summers and warmer during chilly winters. Insulation materials can include foam boards, straw, or even recycled newspapers.

Seasonal Adjustments: Depending on the weather, you may need to adjust ventilation and insulation settings accordingly. For instance, in winter, you can partially close some vents to retain heat while still maintaining proper airflow.

Designing Quail-Friendly Enclosures to Promote Natural Behaviour:

Creating a quail-friendly enclosure means designing a space that encourages the birds to exhibit their natural behaviours. This promotes their overall well-being and ensures they live a fulfilling life:

Nesting Areas: Provide suitable nesting areas for your quail to lay eggs in private and secure spaces. Nesting boxes or containers filled with soft bedding materials, such as straw or wood shavings, will encourage nesting behaviour.

Perches and Roosts: Quail enjoy perching, especially at night. Offer low-level perches or roosts to mimic their natural instinct to perch for safety and comfort.

Dust Bathing Areas: Quail love dust bathing, which helps keep their feathers clean and control parasites. Create a designated dust bathing area with dry soil or sand for them to enjoy this natural behaviour.

Outdoor Access: If possible, allow your quail to have access to an outdoor area where they can forage and experience natural sunlight. This outdoor space should be predator-proof and well-fenced.

Enrichment: Introduce various enrichments, such as hanging treats or toys, to keep your quail mentally stimulated and entertained. Quail love to hide so some cuttings from bushes such as conifers are always welcome.

Conclusion:

In this chapter, we covered the crucial aspects of housing and enclosure setup for quail in the UK. By building or choosing suitable quail housing, ensuring proper ventilation and insulation, and designing quail-friendly enclosures, you will create an environment where your quail can thrive. A well-designed and comfortable housing space will not only promote their natural behaviours but also contribute to their overall health and productivity. Remember to regularly clean and maintain the enclosure to ensure your quail are happy, healthy, and content in their home.

Chapter 4: Nutrition and Feeding Requirements for Quail in the UK

Proper nutrition is fundamental to the health, well-being, and productivity of quail. In this chapter, we explore the essential nutritional needs of quail and provide guidance on formulating a balanced diet that meets their specific requirements. We will discuss the key nutrients necessary for different life stages, the role of supplements, and address common feeding challenges to ensure your quail flock receives optimal nutrition for a vibrant and thriving existence.

Understanding Quail Nutritional Needs:

Quail, like all living organisms, require a balanced diet to support their growth, egg production, and overall health. The nutritional needs of quail vary depending on their age, purpose (egg-laying, meat production, or pets), and environmental conditions. The primary nutrients essential for quail can be categorised as follows:

1. Protein: Protein is the most critical nutrient for quail, especially during growth and egg production. It plays a vital role in muscle development, feather growth, and egg formation. A diet with adequate protein content ensures healthy quail and strong eggshells.

2. Carbohydrates: Carbohydrates provide energy for quail, supporting their daily activities, growth, and egg-laying efforts.

3. Fats: Fats are a concentrated source of energy for quail. They are particularly important during colder months when quail need extra energy to maintain body temperature.

4. Vitamins: Vitamins are essential for various metabolic processes in quail. Vitamin A is crucial for vision, vitamin D aids in calcium absorption, and vitamin E acts as an antioxidant. B-vitamins are also necessary for overall health and well-being.

5. Minerals: Minerals like calcium and phosphorus are essential for eggshell formation and bone health. Other

minerals, such as iron, zinc, and selenium, play vital roles in various physiological functions.

6. Water: Access to clean and fresh water is of utmost importance for quail. Quail requires water for digestion, temperature regulation, and overall hydration.

Formulating a Balanced Diet:

A well-balanced diet ensures that your quail receive all the nutrients they need to thrive. Commercial quail feeds are available and often come in starter, grower, layer, and breeder formulations. However, you can also create a custom diet using a combination of grains, seeds, and commercial feed.

Starter Diet: For newly hatched quail, a high-protein starter diet with around 24-28% protein content is recommended. This diet supports rapid growth and development during the early stages.

Grower Diet: As quail mature, a grower diet with slightly reduced protein content (around 20-24%) is suitable to sustain healthy growth without promoting excessive weight gain.

Layer Diet: When quail reach laying age (around 6-8 weeks for Coturnix quail), they require a layer diet with higher calcium levels (around 18-22%) to support eggshell formation. Layer feeds often include oyster shell or limestone grit to supplement calcium.

Breeder Diet: If you plan to breed your quail, a breeder diet with increased protein and calcium levels (around 20-24% protein and 18-22% calcium) is essential to support egg production and fertility.

Supplements and Treats:

While commercial feeds generally provide a well-balanced diet, you can enhance your quail's nutrition with supplements and occasional treats. Some common supplements and treats include:

Grit: Offering small stones or commercial grit helps quail with digestion by grinding food in their gizzard.

Calcium Supplements: For laying hens, providing additional calcium sources like crushed eggshells or oyster shell can help prevent calcium deficiency and ensure strong eggshells.

Greens and Vegetables: Quail enjoy greens and vegetables like lettuce, spinach, and broccoli. These treats provide added nutrients and mental stimulation.

Mealworms: Dried mealworms are a protein-rich treat that quail find particularly enticing.

Feeding Challenges and Tips:

While providing a balanced diet is essential, quail owners may encounter some feeding challenges:

Overfeeding: Overfeeding can lead to obesity and health problems. Follow recommended feeding guidelines and adjust portions as needed.

Quail can eat a variety of foods, but it's important to provide them with a balanced and appropriate diet to ensure their health and well-being. Here's a list of foods that quail can eat and foods they should avoid:

Foods Quail Can Eat:

1. Commercial Quail Feed: This is formulated to provide the necessary nutrients quail require at different life stages. It's the foundation of their diet.

2. Seeds: Seeds such as millet, sunflower seeds, and various grains are suitable for quail. These can be provided as treats or part of their regular diet.

3. Green Vegetables: Leafy greens like spinach, kale, lettuce, and Swiss chard are rich in vitamins and minerals. Offer a variety of greens for a balanced diet.

4. Vegetables: Carrots, bell peppers, cucumbers, zucchini, and other vegetables can be offered in small quantities.

5. Fruits: Fruits like apples, berries, melons, and grapes can be given occasionally as treats. Avoid high-sugar fruits in excess.

6. Insects and Protein: Insects like mealworms, crickets, and earthworms provide essential protein. These can be particularly important during the breeding season.

7. Cooked Eggs: Hard-boiled or scrambled eggs are a great source of protein and can be offered occasionally.

8. Grains: Cooked rice, oatmeal, and whole grains like barley or quinoa can be part of their diet.

9. Herbs: Parsley, oregano, thyme, and other herbs can be provided in moderation for added flavour and potential health benefits.

Foods Quail Should Avoid:

1. Avocado: Avocado contains a substance called persin that is toxic to birds.

2. Chocolate: Chocolate is toxic to many animals, including quail.

3. Onions and Garlic: These contain compounds that can be harmful to quail and other birds.

4. High-Sugar Foods: Avoid sugary foods like candy or sugary fruits in excess, as they can lead to health issues.

5. Processed Foods: Highly processed and salty foods are not suitable for quail.

6. Caffeine and Alcohol: These should be avoided as they can have negative effects on quail health.

7. Uncooked Beans: Uncooked beans contain compounds that can be toxic, so make sure beans are thoroughly cooked if included.

8. Mouldy or Spoiled Foods: Mouldy or spoiled foods can cause digestive issues and illness.

9. High-Salt Foods: Foods high in salt can be harmful to quail.

10. Dairy: Quail are generally lactose intolerant, so dairy products should be avoided.

Remember that offering a balanced and varied diet is essential for quail health. Commercial quail feed should be the main component of their diet, supplemented with appropriate treats in moderation. Always provide fresh, clean water, and monitor their health and behaviour to ensure they are thriving on the diet you provide. If you're uncertain about a specific food, it's best to consult with a veterinarian or an expert in quail care.

Bullying: In communal feeding situations, some quail may dominate the feeders, preventing others from accessing food. Use multiple feeders to reduce competition.

Environmental Factors: Extreme weather conditions may affect quail's appetite. Adjust feeding schedules and rations accordingly during heatwaves or cold spells.

Conclusion:

Proper nutrition is a cornerstone of successful quail-keeping in the UK. Understanding quail's nutritional needs at different life stages, offering a well-balanced diet, and providing appropriate supplements and treats are vital for their health and productivity. By ensuring your quail receive optimal nutrition, you are fostering a vibrant and thriving flock that will reward you with abundant eggs, healthy meat, and delightful companionship.

Chapter 5: Health Care and Disease Prevention for Quail in the UK

Quail, like all animals, require attentive health care and disease prevention measures to thrive in their environment. In this chapter, we delve into common health issues specific to quail in the UK, discuss how to recognise signs of illness, and explore when to seek veterinary care. Additionally, we emphasise the critical importance of implementing biosecurity measures to prevent disease outbreaks and safeguard the well-being of your quail flock. We'll also explore natural alternative treatments that can complement or supplement conventional veterinary care.

Common Health Issues Specific to Quail in the UK:

1. Respiratory Issues: Quail can be susceptible to respiratory problems, particularly in damp or poorly ventilated environments. Signs of respiratory issues may include sneezing, coughing, nasal discharge, and laboured breathing.

Natural Alternative Treatment: Improving ventilation in the quail housing can help reduce respiratory issues. You can also add herbs like thyme, oregano, or garlic to their diet, as they have natural antibacterial and antiviral properties that may support respiratory health.

2. Egg-Laying Problems: Some quail may experience egg-laying difficulties, such as egg binding, where an egg gets stuck in the reproductive tract. This condition can be life-threatening and requires immediate attention.

Natural Alternative Treatment: Providing quail with calcium supplements and offering ample natural sources of calcium, such as crushed eggshells or oyster shells, may help prevent egg-laying issues.

3. Coccidiosis: Coccidiosis is a common intestinal parasitic infection in quail and other poultry. It is caused by protozoa and can lead to diarrhoea, decreased appetite, and weakness.

Natural Alternative Treatment: Certain herbs like wormwood and thyme have shown potential in combating coccidiosis. Consult with a veterinarian or herbalist for appropriate dosage and administration.

4. Mites and Lice: External parasites like mites and lice can infest quail and cause irritation, feather loss, and anaemia. Regular inspections and appropriate treatments are essential to manage these infestations.

Natural Alternative Treatment: Diatomaceous earth can be used as a natural insecticide to control mites and lice. Sprinkle it in the quail housing and dusting areas to help eliminate parasites.

5. Nutritional Deficiencies: Inadequate nutrition can lead to health issues, such as poor feather quality, decreased egg production, and weak bones. Properly balanced diets are crucial to prevent nutritional deficiencies.

Natural Alternative Treatment: Adding herbs like nettle, dandelion, and chickweed to the quail's diet can provide additional nutrients and support overall health.

6. Foot and Leg Problems: Overgrown toenails or injuries can cause foot and leg problems in quail. Affected birds may have difficulty walking and may become lethargic.

Natural Alternative Treatment: Regularly trimming overgrown toenails and providing a soft and comfortable bedding material can help prevent foot and leg issues.

Recognising Signs of Illness and When to Seek Veterinary Care:

Observing your quail regularly and knowing how to recognise signs of illness is crucial for prompt intervention. If you notice any of the following signs, it is essential to seek veterinary care:

- Unusual lethargy or listlessness
- Loss of appetite or decreased water intake

- Difficulty breathing
- Changes in vocalisation or abnormal noises
- Abnormal droppings (diarrhoea, blood, or mucus)
- Limping or difficulty moving
- Discharge from the eyes or nostrils
- Abnormal feather loss or changes in feather quality
- Prolonged cessation of egg-laying in mature hens
- Visible parasites on the body or feathers

Natural Alternative Treatment: For mild symptoms or as a complementary approach, you can try providing immune-boosting herbs like echinacea or elderberry. However, always consult with a veterinarian for serious or persistent health issues.

Implementing Biosecurity Measures to Prevent Disease Outbreaks:

Biosecurity is a set of practices designed to prevent the introduction and spread of infectious diseases in quail flocks. Implementing biosecurity measures is crucial for both small-scale and commercial quail keepers to protect their birds' health and maintain a disease-free environment. Here are some key biosecurity practices:

1. Quarantine: Always quarantine new quail before introducing them to your existing flock. Isolating new birds for at least two weeks allows you to observe them for signs of illness before they interact with the main flock.

2. Controlled Access: Restrict access to your quail enclosure to essential personnel only. If you visit other poultry farms or aviaries, change clothes and footwear before entering your quail area to minimise the risk of bringing in contaminants.

3. Cleanliness and Disinfection: Keep the quail housing and surrounding areas clean at all times. Regularly disinfect feeders, waterers, and equipment to prevent the buildup of pathogens.

Natural Alternative Treatment: Certain essential oils, such as tea tree oil or eucalyptus oil, have natural antimicrobial properties and can be used in cleaning solutions for the quail housing.

4. Rodent and Wild Bird Control: Rodents and wild birds can carry diseases and parasites that may affect quail. Implement measures to deter or eliminate their presence in and around the quail enclosure.

Natural Alternative Treatment: You can use natural deterrents like peppermint oil or install owl boxes to control rodent and bird populations.

5. Avoid Sharing Equipment: Do not share equipment, such as feeders or waterers, with other poultry keepers to prevent cross-contamination.

6. Footbaths and Hand Washing: Use footbaths containing a disinfectant at entry and exit points to reduce the risk of spreading diseases. Additionally, practice thorough hand washing before and after handling quail.

7. Observation and Record Keeping: Regularly observe your quail for signs of illness and maintain accurate records of any

health issues. This helps track patterns and identify potential disease outbreaks early on.

Conclusion:

Proactive health care and disease prevention are essential aspects of responsible quail keeping in the UK. Being familiar with common health issues, recognising signs of illness, and seeking veterinary care when necessary are critical for maintaining a healthy and thriving quail flock. Natural alternative treatments can complement or supplement conventional veterinary care and may be beneficial for mild symptoms or as preventive measures. By implementing stringent biosecurity measures, including natural alternatives, you can minimise the risk of disease outbreaks and provide a safe and nurturing environment for your quail, ensuring they lead long, happy, and disease-free lives. Always consult with a veterinarian for serious or persistent health issues to ensure the best care for your quail.

Chapter 6: Breeding and Incubation in the UK

Breeding Strategies for Successful Reproduction

Breeding quail successfully requires careful planning and consideration of various factors. One of the crucial steps is selecting healthy and genetically diverse quail as breeding stock. Avoid inbreeding by choosing birds that are not closely related. Look for traits like good egg-laying performance, early maturity, and desirable meat quality in your selected breeders.

Maintaining a Suitable Breeding Ratio: Achieving successful breeding outcomes in quail populations relies heavily on maintaining a suitable breeding ratio. A recommended breeding ratio is typically one male quail to every three to five female quails. This ratio has been observed to contribute to optimal fertility rates while also addressing the social dynamics within the group. With this ratio, each female receives adequate attention from the male, reducing the potential for over mating and minimising stress on the hens.

For instance, if you have a quail flock consisting of 15 females, a well-balanced breeding group would ideally include 3 to 5 male quails. This arrangement not only ensures that the males are not overwhelmed with mating duties but also allows the females to experience more controlled interactions with the males, which can lead to improved breeding success.

Choosing Between Natural Mating and Artificial Insemination: When it comes to the breeding process, quail owners must consider whether to allow natural mating or employ artificial insemination. Natural mating is a common method, especially in small-scale quail operations. However, in certain scenarios, such as breeding valuable genetic lines or addressing fertility challenges, artificial insemination might become necessary.

For example, if you're working with a quail strain that carries specific genetic traits you want to preserve, artificial insemination provides a controlled way to ensure the desired genetic makeup is passed on without relying solely on the chance encounters of natural mating. Similarly, if fertility issues arise within the flock, artificial insemination can be a valuable tool to address those challenges and enhance breeding success rates.

Encouraging Nesting Behaviour: To foster successful breeding, providing appropriate nesting boxes with soft and comfortable bedding materials is crucial. These nesting boxes offer quail females a designated space to lay their eggs, encouraging natural nesting behaviours and reducing stress. The presence of soft bedding materials mimics the natural environment and creates a cosy space for egg laying.

Privacy in the Breeding Area: Quails are sensitive creatures, and stress can significantly impact their breeding success. Ensuring that the breeding area offers privacy is paramount. Quail breeding enclosures should be designed in a way that minimises disturbances and distractions. This can be achieved by using dividers, barriers, or vegetation to create secluded and tranquil areas where quails can engage in their breeding behaviours without unnecessary stressors.

For instance, if you're breeding quails in an indoor environment, you can arrange nesting boxes in a way that they are shielded from direct view and human activity. In an outdoor setup, consider incorporating natural vegetation or artificial structures that create secluded spaces where quails can engage in breeding behaviours away from the prying eyes of potential stressors.

In conclusion, successful quail breeding involves careful attention to breeding ratios, consideration of the appropriate breeding method, provision of suitable nesting environments, and creating stress-free spaces for breeding activities. By implementing these strategies, quail owners can enhance the likelihood of breeding success, produce healthy offspring, and contribute positively to the overall sustainability of their quail population.

Seasonal Considerations for Breeding in the UK

The breeding season for quail can be year-round, but seasonal considerations can influence success and productivity.

Spring and summer are ideal for breeding quail in the UK due to longer daylight hours and milder temperatures. The increase in daylight triggers hormonal responses in quail, encouraging them to lay more eggs and exhibit breeding behaviours.

Autumn breeding is possible, but egg production may decline due to reduced daylight hours. To sustain egg-laying in autumn, consider using artificial lighting to mimic longer days. However, artificial light can have a long term detrimental effect on quail.

Breeding in winter can be challenging, as quail tend to lay fewer eggs during colder and darker months. If breeding in winter, provide ample artificial lighting to maintain a consistent day length and stimulate egg production.

Incubation Techniques and Best Practices

Quail hens can be excellent natural incubators. Allow them to incubate their eggs in a quiet and safe environment. Provide proper nesting materials and ensure they have access to food and water without disturbing their nest.

Using an incubator is a common method for hatching quail eggs. Set the incubator to the appropriate temperature (around 37.5°C or 99.5°F) and humidity (approximately 50-60%) for quail eggs. Turn the eggs regularly during the incubation period to promote proper development.

Quail eggs typically hatch in 16-18 days. Monitor the temperature and humidity levels throughout the incubation period to ensure successful hatching.

Candling is a technique used to assess the development of the embryos inside the eggs. It involves shining a bright light through the egg to see the contents. Remove any infertile or non-developing eggs to prevent contamination.

Create a warm and protected brooding environment for the quail chicks once they hatch. Prepare a brooder with a heat lamp or heat pad to keep the chicks warm for the first few weeks of their lives.

Chapter 7: Maximising Quail Egg Production in the UK

Tips for Optimising Egg Production in the UK Climate

Ensuring a consistent and abundant supply of quail eggs requires careful attention to their diet, lighting, housing, and overall well-being. Here are some detailed tips to maximise quail egg production in the UK climate:

1. Well-Balanced Diet:
Quail, like all birds, require a well-balanced and nutrient-rich diet to support optimal egg production. Commercial quail feed or specially formulated diets for layers are readily available and provide essential nutrients, including protein, calcium, and vitamins, necessary for healthy hens and robust egg production. Consider supplementing their diet with fresh greens, such as spinach, kale, and dandelion leaves, to provide additional nutrients and variety.

2. Daylight Length and Artificial Lighting:
Quail are sensitive to daylight length, and the duration of daylight greatly influences their reproductive hormones,

which, in turn, impacts their egg-laying. In the UK, where daylight hours vary with the seasons, egg production tends to decline during the darker winter months. To sustain egg production year-round, consider using artificial lighting in the quail housing. Provide at least 14-16 hours of light per day using timers to simulate longer days and encourage continued egg-laying. However, as mentioned previously, artificial light can have a detrimental effect on quail and shorten their life.

3. Stress-Free Housing Environment:
Stress can have a negative impact on egg production, so it is crucial to create a calm and comfortable living environment for your quail. Ensure the housing is well-ventilated to maintain proper airflow and prevent ammonia buildup. Keep the housing clean and free from pests or predators that can cause stress to the birds. Providing nesting boxes for the hens to lay their eggs privately can reduce stress and encourage more consistent egg-laying.

4. Temperature and Humidity Control:

Quail are sensitive to temperature extremes, which can affect their egg production and overall health. Ensure the quail housing maintains appropriate temperature and humidity levels. During the colder months, consider using heat lamps or providing insulation to keep the birds warm. In contrast, during hot weather, ensure adequate ventilation and access to shade to prevent heat stress.

5. Ample Fresh Water:

Quail, like all animals, need a constant supply of fresh water to stay hydrated and healthy. During the egg-laying period, their water needs may increase, so ensure easy access to clean water at all times. Consider using nipple drinkers or water containers that minimise spillage and keep the water clean.

Extending the Laying Season through Husbandry Practices

1. Artificial Lighting in Winter:

As mentioned earlier, introducing artificial lighting to extend daylight hours during the darker winter months can help sustain egg production. Gradually increase the hours of artificial light in the evening, providing a consistent and predictable schedule for the quail.

2. Managing Moulting:

Quail may undergo a moulting phase, during which they shed and replace their feathers. Moulting can temporarily interrupt egg-laying, as the energy and nutrients are redirected towards feather growth. Providing proper nutrition during this period can support a quicker moult and faster return to egg production. Supplement their diet with additional protein and calcium-rich foods to aid feather regrowth.

3. Introducing Young Hens:

As older hens' egg production naturally declines with age, introducing young hens into the flock can help maintain a steady supply of eggs. Young hens are typically more prolific layers and can help compensate for any decrease in egg production from older birds.

Handling and Storing Quail Eggs for Freshness

1. Gentle Egg Collection:

Collect quail eggs regularly to prevent them from getting dirty or damaged. Use a gentle touch when handling the eggs to avoid cracking or breaking the delicate shells.

2. Avoid Washing Eggs:

Quail eggs, like chicken eggs, have a natural protective coating called the bloom, which helps maintain freshness and prevents the entry of bacteria. Avoid washing quail eggs, as doing so removes the protective coating. Instead, only wipe off any dirt or debris with a dry cloth if necessary.

3. Proper Egg Storage:

Store quail eggs in a cool and dry place with a stable temperature of around 10-15°C (50-59°F). A consistent temperature prevents fluctuations that can lead to spoilage. You can use an egg carton or an egg storage container to help keep the eggs upright and protect them from damage.

4. Freshness and Shelf Life:

Quail eggs have a shorter shelf life compared to chicken eggs. When stored correctly, quail eggs can stay fresh for up to three weeks. To determine their freshness, conduct the float test. Place an egg in a bowl of water; if it sinks and lies flat, it is fresh. If it stands upright or floats, it may not be as fresh and should be used promptly.

By implementing these tips and practices, you can maximise quail egg production in the UK climate, ensuring a steady supply of nutritious and delicious eggs from your quail flock. With proper care and attention, your quail will thrive and continue to provide you with fresh and healthy eggs year-round.

Chapter 8: Utilising Quail Meat in the UK

Humanely Raising Quail for Meat in the UK

Raising quail for meat in the UK is a responsible and ethical practice when done with the birds' welfare in mind. Providing a humane and comfortable environment for the quail is paramount. Ensure that they have ample space to move around and engage in natural behaviours. While quail can be kept in cages, consider offering them more space in aviaries or pens, allowing them to fly and explore. A stress-free and enriched environment can contribute to healthier and tastier meat.

Proper nutrition plays a significant role in the quality of quail meat. A well-balanced diet is essential for the birds' growth and overall health. Commercially available quail feed can be supplemented with greens, seeds, and insects, providing a more natural and varied diet. Additionally, ensuring a steady supply of clean, fresh water is vital for their well-being.

Slaughtering and Processing Quail for the Table

When it is time to harvest quail for meat, it must be done humanely and efficiently. Humane slaughter methods prioritise the birds' welfare and ensure a quick and painless process. One method is cervical dislocation, where the neck is swiftly and accurately broken, causing immediate death. This technique can be performed by experienced handlers, or you can seek the assistance of a professional veterinarian or a trained poultry processor.

After slaughtering, the birds should be properly processed to ensure food safety and quality. The process involves carefully plucking feathers, removing the internal organs, and cleaning the carcass thoroughly. Proper sanitation and hygiene are crucial during this stage to prevent contamination. If you are new to processing quail, it is advisable to seek guidance from experienced poultry processors or attend workshops to learn proper techniques.

Preparing Traditional and Innovative Quail Meat Dishes

Quail meat's versatility makes it a favourite among chefs and home cooks alike. Its delicate, tender texture and rich flavour lend themselves to a wide range of culinary creations. Here are a few traditional and innovative quail meat dishes that you can try in your kitchen:

1. Grilled Quail with Rosemary and Lemon

Ingredients:
- 4 quail, cleaned and dressed
- 2 tablespoons olive oil
- 2 cloves garlic, minced
- 1 tablespoon fresh rosemary, chopped
- Zest of 1 lemon
- Salt and pepper to taste
- Fresh lemon wedges for serving

Instructions:
- Preheat the grill to medium-high heat.
- In a bowl, mix the olive oil, minced garlic, chopped rosemary, lemon zest, salt, and pepper.

- Rub the quail with the marinade, ensuring they are evenly coated.
- Grill the quail for about 4-5 minutes on each side or until the internal temperature reaches 165°F (74°C).
- Serve the grilled quail with fresh lemon wedges for an extra burst of flavour.

2. Quail Adobo

Ingredients:
- 4 quail, cleaned and dressed
- 1/4 cup soy sauce
- 1/4 cup vinegar
- 4 cloves garlic, minced
- 2 bay leaves
- 1/2 teaspoon black peppercorns
- 2 tablespoons cooking oil
- Cooked rice for serving

Instructions:
- In a bowl, mix the soy sauce, vinegar, minced garlic, bay leaves, and black peppercorns.

- Add the quail to the marinade and let them marinate for at least 30 minutes.
- In a pan, heat the cooking oil over medium heat. Sear the quail on all sides until golden brown.
- Pour the marinade into the pan and bring it to a simmer.
- Cover the pan and let the quail cook for about 20-25 minutes or until tender and fully cooked.
- Serve the quail adobo with steamed rice for a delicious and comforting meal.

3. Quail and Mushroom Risotto

Ingredients:
- 4 quail breasts, boneless and skinless
- 1 cup arborio rice
- 4 cups chicken broth
- 1/2 cup white wine
- 1 small onion, finely chopped
- 2 cups mushrooms, sliced
- 2 tablespoons butter
- 1/2 cup grated Parmesan cheese
- Salt and pepper to taste

- Fresh parsley for garnish

Instructions:

- Season the quail breasts with salt and pepper. In a pan, heat a little oil and cook the quail breasts until they are golden brown and cooked through. Set aside.
- In a separate pot, heat the chicken broth and keep it warm over low heat.
- In the same pan used for the quail, sauté the chopped onion until translucent. Add the arborio rice and stir to coat it with the onion.
- Pour in the white wine and cook until it is absorbed by the rice.
- Gradually add the warm chicken broth, one ladle at a time, stirring constantly and allowing the liquid to be absorbed before adding more.
- When the rice is cooked and creamy, stir in the sliced mushrooms and cooked quail breasts.
- Finish the risotto by stirring in the butter and grated Parmesan cheese.
- Serve the quail and mushroom risotto garnished with fresh parsley for a delightful and comforting meal.

4. Quail Tacos

Ingredients:
- 4 quail, cleaned and dressed
- 1 tablespoon olive oil
- 1 teaspoon chili powder
- 1/2 teaspoon cumin
- 1/2 teaspoon paprika
- 1/2 teaspoon garlic powder
- Salt and pepper to taste
- 8 small tortillas
- Salsa, guacamole, and fresh cilantro for serving

Instructions:
- Preheat the oven to 375°F (190°C).
- In a bowl, mix the olive oil, chili powder, cumin, paprika, garlic powder, salt, and pepper.
- Rub the quail with the spice mixture, ensuring they are evenly coated.
- Place the quail on a baking sheet and roast in the oven for about 15-20 minutes or until fully cooked.

- Remove the quail from the oven and let them rest for a few minutes.
- Shred the quail meat and assemble the tacos with the tortillas, salsa, guacamole, and fresh cilantro.

5. Quail with Red Wine Reduction

Ingredients:
- 4 quail, cleaned and dressed
- 1 cup red wine
- 1/2 cup chicken broth
- 2 shallots, finely chopped
- 2 cloves garlic, minced
- 2 sprigs fresh thyme
- 2 tablespoons butter
- Salt and pepper to taste

Instructions:
- Season the quail with salt and pepper. In a pan, melt a tablespoon of butter and cook the quail over medium heat until they are golden brown and cooked through. Set aside.

- In the same pan, add the chopped shallots and minced garlic. Sauté until they are softened and fragrant.
- Pour in the red wine and bring it to a simmer. Scrape any browned bits from the bottom of the pan.
- Add the chicken broth and fresh thyme to the pan. Let the sauce reduce by half.
- Stir in the remaining tablespoon of butter to create a rich and glossy sauce.
- Serve the quail with the red wine reduction sauce

for an elegant and flavourful dish.

Enjoy the delightful experience of exploring quail meat in your kitchen with these delicious recipes. Whether you opt for traditional preparations or innovative dishes, quail meat's tenderness and delectable flavour are sure to impress. Remember to prioritise humane and responsible practices when raising quail for meat, ensuring the birds' welfare and the quality of the end product. Bon appétit!

Chapter 9: Quail as Pets and Educational Resources

Quail as Pets in the UK: Care and Interaction

Quail can make wonderful and endearing pets for those seeking a unique and rewarding pet-keeping experience. Their small size, gentle nature, and delightful behaviours make them suitable for families, individuals, and even urban dwellers with limited space. However, it is essential to provide them with proper care and attention to ensure they lead happy and healthy lives.

Housing and Environment:
When keeping quail as pets, it is crucial to provide them with a suitable and comfortable living environment. An indoor or outdoor aviary with ample space is ideal, as it allows the quail to move, forage, and engage in natural behaviours. Ensure the enclosure is secure and protected from predators, and offer appropriate shelter from harsh weather conditions.

Social Interaction:

Quail are sociable birds and enjoy the company of their own kind. Consider keeping them in pairs or small groups to prevent loneliness and promote a sense of well-being. Interacting with your quail regularly can also help build trust and strengthen the bond between you and your feathered companions.

Feeding and Nutrition:
A well-balanced diet is essential for the health and vitality of pet quail. Commercial quail feed is readily available and serves as the foundation of their diet. Supplement their meals with fresh greens, seeds, and insects to offer them a more varied and natural diet. Ensure they have access to clean, fresh water at all times.

Handling and Taming:
Gentle and patient handling is key to taming quail and making them comfortable around humans. Start by offering treats from your hand and gradually introducing touch. Avoid sudden movements or loud noises, as quail can be skittish. With time and positive reinforcement, many quail can become tame and enjoy human interaction.

Incorporating Quail into Educational Programs and School Projects

Quail offer valuable educational opportunities, making them excellent additions to schools and educational programs. Their life cycle, reproductive behaviour, and unique characteristics provide valuable lessons in various subjects:

Biology Lessons:
Quail's reproductive cycle, from incubation to hatching, offers a hands-on and engaging way for students to learn about animal reproduction and embryonic development. Observing the eggs in an incubator and witnessing the chicks hatch fosters a deeper understanding of biology concepts.

Agriculture and Sustainability:
Integrating quail-keeping into school projects can teach students about sustainable agriculture and responsible animal husbandry. Students can learn how to provide the necessary care for quail, manage their living environment,

and promote their well-being while considering ethical and environmental implications.

Responsibility and Compassion:
Caring for quail fosters a sense of responsibility and compassion in students. By taking on the role of caregivers, students learn about the importance of meeting the needs of animals and the impact of responsible pet ownership.

Promoting Awareness of Quail as a Sustainable Option in the UK

Raising quail for eggs and meat offers a sustainable and ethical alternative to traditional poultry farming. By promoting awareness of quail as a viable option, we can encourage more individuals and communities to embrace this eco-friendly practice:

Nutritional Benefits:
Quail eggs are rich in protein, vitamins, and minerals, making them a nutritious addition to the diet. Advocating for quail

eggs as a healthy and sustainable protein source can help address food security and nutrition challenges.

Lower Environmental Impact:

Compared to larger poultry, quail require less space, feed, and resources to thrive. Raising quail on a small scale has a lower environmental impact, making it an attractive option for eco-conscious individuals and communities.

Educating Consumers:

Educating consumers about the benefits of quail products can lead to increased demand and support for sustainable quail-keeping practices. Highlighting the humane treatment of quail and their positive impact on the environment can influence purchasing decisions.

Supporting Local Producers:

Supporting local quail farmers and producers can foster sustainable and ethical agriculture practices within communities. Choosing locally sourced quail products helps promote a more resilient and sustainable food system.

Conclusion:

Quail, whether kept as pets or incorporated into educational programs, have much to offer in terms of companionship, learning opportunities, and sustainable practices. By providing them with proper care and attention as pets and using them as educational resources, we can foster a deeper understanding of animal welfare and responsible agriculture practices. Additionally, promoting quail as a sustainable option in the UK can lead to more environmentally conscious food choices and support for local farmers. Embracing quail-keeping and raising awareness about its benefits can contribute to a more sustainable and compassionate future for both humans and our feathered friends.

Chapter 10: Troubleshooting and FAQs for UK Quail Keepers

Addressing Common Challenges Faced by UK Quail Keepers

Quail keeping may come with certain challenges, such as health issues, environmental concerns, and predator threats. Address these challenges proactively to ensure the well-being of your quail.

Frequently Asked Questions and Practical Solutions for UK Quail Keepers

1. How many quail should I start with as a beginner?

Practical Solution: As a beginner, start with a small flock of 4 to 6 quail. This manageable number allows you to gain experience in quail keeping without being overwhelmed. Once you are comfortable with their care and management, you can consider expanding your flock.

2. How much space do quail need?

Practical Solution: Quail require at least 1 square foot of space per bird. For a small flock, a coop or enclosure measuring 4 square feet is sufficient. However, if possible, provide more space to allow the quail to move and express natural behaviours freely.

3. What should I feed my quail?

Practical Solution: Quail thrive on commercial quail feed or specially formulated diets for layers. These feeds contain essential nutrients, vitamins, and minerals required for their health and optimal egg production. You can supplement their diet with fresh greens, vegetables, and occasional treats like mealworms or fruits.

4. How do I prevent egg-eating behaviour in my quail?

Practical Solution: Egg-eating behaviour can develop if quail accidentally break an egg, and they discover that the contents are a tasty treat. To prevent this, use deep, cushioned nesting boxes filled with clean bedding material. Collect eggs frequently to reduce the chances of breakage, and provide a calcium supplement to meet their dietary needs and reduce the temptation to eat their own eggs.

5. Can I keep different quail species together?

Practical Solution: It is generally not recommended to keep different quail species together, as they may have different dietary requirements and behaviours. Mixing species can lead to stress, aggression, and potential health issues. If you wish to keep multiple quail species, provide separate enclosures or aviaries for each species.

6. How can I sex quail to ensure I have a balanced flock?

Practical Solution: Sexing quail can be challenging, especially in young birds. The most reliable method is to observe their vocalisations and physical characteristics once they mature. Males usually have a more pronounced and repetitive call, while females are quieter and have a more refined appearance. If you want a balanced flock, consider purchasing sexed day-old chicks from a reputable breeder.

7. How do I prevent and control common health issues in quail?

Practical Solution: Maintaining a clean and well-ventilated housing environment is essential for preventing common health issues in quail. Regularly inspect your birds for signs of illness, such as lethargy, loss of appetite, or abnormal droppings. Quarantine new birds before introducing them to the flock to prevent the spread of diseases. In case of illness, consult a veterinarian experienced in treating poultry or explore natural remedies such as garlic or oregano oil, which are known for their antibacterial properties.

8. How can I incubate quail eggs successfully?

Practical Solution: To successfully incubate quail eggs, maintain a stable temperature between 37.5°C to 38.5°C (99.5°F to 101.3°F) and a humidity level of 50-60%. Turn the eggs gently at least three times a day to prevent the embryo from sticking to the shell. Incubation typically takes 17 to 18 days. After hatching, keep the chicks in a brooder with a heat lamp and clean bedding until they are fully feathered.

9. How can I introduce new quail to an existing flock?

Practical Solution: Introducing new quail to an existing flock requires caution to prevent aggression and stress. Use a separate enclosure within the main coop or run, allowing the birds to see and interact with each other without physical contact. After a few days, if they seem calm and accepting, you can gradually integrate the new birds into the main flock during daytime hours when supervision is possible.

10. How do I protect my quail from predators?

Practical Solution: Protecting your quail from predators is vital. Use secure and sturdy fencing around the coop and run, burying it partially underground to prevent burrowing predators. Install locks and latches on doors to ensure they cannot be opened easily. Consider using motion-activated lights or alarms to deter nocturnal predators.

By addressing these frequently asked questions and providing practical solutions, UK quail keepers can navigate common challenges and ensure a successful and rewarding experience in raising quail. Remember that every quail flock is unique, so being attentive to their specific needs and behaviours will lead to happier, healthier birds.

Conclusion

By understanding breeding and incubation techniques, optimising egg production, humanely raising quail for meat, and utilising quail as pets and educational resources, UK quail keepers can create a thriving and sustainable quail-keeping experience. Addressing common challenges and providing practical solutions ensures that quail keepers can overcome obstacles and enjoy the benefits of these captivating birds.

In this comprehensive guide to quail keeping in the UK, we have explored the fascinating world of these small, captivating birds and their rising popularity among poultry enthusiasts. Quail offer a wealth of benefits, making them an ideal choice for a diverse range of individuals, from hobbyists seeking a rewarding pastime to homesteaders looking for a sustainable source of eggs and meat.

Throughout the chapters, we have covered various aspects of quail keeping, providing valuable insights and practical advice for success:

Chapter 1: Understanding Quail Species Suitable for the UK

We explored the common quail species raised in the UK, such as Coturnix quail, Bobwhite quail, and California quail. Each species brings its unique attributes and requirements, allowing quail keepers to tailor their experience to suit their preferences and specific purposes.

Chapter 2: Legalities and Regulations in the UK

We emphasised the importance of compliance with legal requirements and obtaining necessary permits and licenses, where applicable. Upholding animal welfare standards and best practices is essential to ensure the well-being of quail and contribute to environmental sustainability.

Chapter 3: Housing and Enclosure Setup for Quail in the UK

We discussed the significance of providing suitable and comfortable housing environments for quail. Proper ventilation, insulation, and designing quail-friendly enclosures promote the birds' well-being and encourage their natural behaviours.

Chapter 4: Nutrition and Feeding Requirements for Quail in the UK.

We highlighted the importance of a balanced diet to ensure the health and productivity of quail. Additionally, we explored natural alternative treatments for common health issues, emphasising the role of proper nutrition in disease prevention.

Chapter 5: Health Care and Disease Prevention

We discussed common health issues specific to quail in the UK and provided insights into recognising signs of illness and when to seek veterinary care. Implementing biosecurity measures was emphasised to prevent disease outbreaks and protect the quail flock.

Chapter 6: Breeding and Incubation in the UK

We covered breeding strategies for successful reproduction, seasonal considerations for breeding, and incubation techniques. These insights are crucial for those interested in expanding their quail flock through natural reproduction or artificial incubation.

Chapter 7: Maximising Quail Egg Production

We provided tips for optimising egg production in the UK climate and extending the laying season through husbandry practices. Proper handling and storing of quail eggs ensure their freshness and nutritional value.

Chapter 8: Utilising Quail Meat in the UK

We explored humane methods for raising quail for meat, as well as slaughtering and processing techniques. Additionally, we offered ideas for preparing traditional and innovative quail meat dishes.

Chapter 9: Quail as Pets and Educational Resources

We discussed the care and interaction required when keeping quail as pets in the UK. Furthermore, we explored the potential of incorporating quail into educational programs and school projects to promote awareness of quail as a sustainable option.

Chapter 10: Troubleshooting and FAQs for UK Quail Keepers

We addressed common challenges faced by UK quail keepers and provided practical solutions to overcome these obstacles. Additionally, we answered frequently asked questions to support quail enthusiasts on their journey.

In conclusion, quail keeping in the UK is a rewarding and diverse endeavour that caters to a wide range of interests and purposes. Whether you're looking to enjoy quail as delightful pets, savour their nutritious eggs and flavourful meat, or engage in sustainable and ethical poultry practices, this guide equips you with the knowledge and confidence to embark on a successful quail-keeping adventure. By prioritising the well-being of your quail and following best practices, you can create a thriving and fulfilling experience for both you and your feathered companions. Embrace the fascinating world of quail keeping and unlock the countless rewards these captivating birds have to offer in the United Kingdom.

I trust that this book has provided you with a wealth of information that will prove to be both enlightening and valuable in your endeavours to care for and maintain your quail. The intention behind its content is to furnish you with a comprehensive understanding of the nuances involved in quail husbandry, equipping you with the knowledge and skills necessary to ensure the well-being and thriving of your quail flock. By delving into the pages of this book, I am optimistic that you have gained insights that will empower you to navigate the intricacies of quail care adeptly, fostering an environment that is conducive to their health, happiness, and productivity. Your dedication to learning and applying these insights bodes well for the future of your quail-raising journey, and I have high hopes that the guidance provided within these pages will stand as a valuable resource as you embark on this fulfilling endeavour.

Appendix: Useful Contacts and Links

1. The British Poultry Council (BPC)

Website: https://www.britishpoultry.org.uk

The BPC is the representative body for the British poultry meat sector. They provide valuable information and resources for poultry keepers, including quail keepers, in the UK.

2. RSPCA

Website: https://www.rspca.org.uk

The Royal Society for the Prevention of Cruelty to Animals (RSPCA) is the leading animal welfare charity in the UK. They offer guidance on responsible animal keeping and can provide advice on the welfare of quail.

3. Department for Environment, Food & Rural Affairs (DEFRA)

Website:

https://www.gov.uk/government/organisations/department-for-environment-food-rural-affairs

DEFRA is the UK government department responsible for safeguarding the natural environment and supporting the agricultural sector. They provide information on animal welfare regulations and relevant permits.

4. Animal and Plant Health Agency (APHA)

Website:

https://www.gov.uk/government/organisations/animal-and-plant-health-agency

The APHA is responsible for safeguarding animal and plant health in the UK. They offer guidance on preventing and controlling animal diseases, including those that may affect quail.

5. The Poultry Site

Website: https://www.thepoultrysite.com

The Poultry Site is a comprehensive online resource for all things poultry-related. It includes articles, forums, and news updates relevant to quail keepers in the UK.

6. Country Smallholding Magazine

Website: https://www.countrysmallholding.com

Country Smallholding is a magazine and online platform that caters to small-scale farmers, homesteaders, and poultry keepers. It offers valuable advice and insights for quail enthusiasts in the UK.

7. The British Veterinary Poultry Association (BVPA)

Website: https://www.bvpa.org.uk

The BVPA is an organisation dedicated to promoting avian health and welfare. They have a directory of avian veterinarians who can provide specialised care for quail.

8. Local Quail Keepers' Associations and Forums

Engaging with local quail keepers' associations and online forums can provide valuable support and information from experienced quail enthusiasts in your area. Search for regional groups or join online communities dedicated to quail keeping.

Please note that the contact details and links provided are based on information available up to 2023. Ensure that you verify the information and check for any updates or changes to the websites and contact details. Additionally, always seek advice from reputable sources and professionals when it comes to quail health, welfare, and legal requirements in the UK.

Glossary of terms relevant to quail keeping in the UK:

1. Aviary: An outdoor enclosure designed to provide a spacious and natural environment for quail, allowing them to engage in more natural behaviours.

2. Brooder: A heated enclosure or area where newly hatched quail chicks are kept to maintain optimal temperature and conditions for their initial growth.

3. Candling: The process of using a bright light source to inspect the development of embryos within quail eggs to determine viability.

4. Coturnix Quail: Also known as Japanese quail, this is one of the most common quail species kept for egg and meat production in the UK.

5. Dusting Area: A designated space within the quail enclosure where dust baths can be taken to help control external parasites and maintain feather health.

6. Egg Candling: The practice of holding a light to quail eggs to check for fertility, embryo development, and overall egg quality.

7. Free-Range: Allowing quail to have access to outdoor areas where they can forage and exhibit natural behaviours.

8. Grit: Small, coarse particles or stones provided to quail to aid in digestion by grinding down food in their gizzard.

9. Incubation: The process of artificially maintaining the temperature and humidity levels required for quail eggs to hatch.

10. Jumbo Quail: A selectively bred larger variant of the Coturnix quail, often raised for meat production due to its size.

11. Moult: The natural shedding and replacement of feathers that occurs periodically in quail, often leading to a temporary decrease in egg production.

12. Pullet: A young female quail that has not yet reached egg-laying maturity.

13. Quail Run: A designated enclosed area where quail can roam, forage, and exercise safely.

14. Roosting Bars: Elevated perches or bars within the quail enclosure where quail can rest and sleep comfortably.

15. Scratch Area: A part of the enclosure where quail are encouraged to scratch and forage for insects, seeds, and vegetation.

16. Sexing: Determining the gender of quail, which is important for managing flock dynamics and egg production.

17. Treadle Feeder: A feeder designed with a mechanism that opens when quail step on a platform, preventing wild birds and rodents from accessing the feed.

18. Ventilation: Adequate air circulation within the quail housing to maintain good air quality and prevent humidity buildup.

19. Wing Clipping: The practice of trimming the flight feathers of quail to prevent them from flying over fences or escaping their enclosure.

20. Yolk Sac: A nutrient-rich sac attached to the embryo inside a quail egg, providing nourishment during the early stages of development.

This glossary should help you navigate the terminology and concepts related to quail keeping in the UK.

Printed in Great Britain
by Amazon

41739384R00066